SYMONS & MITCHELLS'

VICTORIAN
NAVAL
MISCELLANY

SYMONS & MITCHELLS'
VICTORIAN NAVAL MISCELLANY

The Naval & Military Press

Published by

The Naval & Military Press Ltd
Unit 5 Riverside, Brambleside
Bellbrook Industrial Estate
Uckfield, East Sussex
TN22 1QQ England

Tel: +44 (0)1825 749494

www.naval-military-press.com
www.nmarchive.com

In reprinting in facsimile from the original, any imperfections are inevitably reproduced and the quality may fall short of modern type and cartographic standards.

Her Majesty's Navy.

THE LOOK OUT.

VOL. I.

HER MAJESTY'S NAVY

With Coloured Illustrations

By W. CHRISTIAN SYMONS and W. FRED. MITCHELL

VOLUME 1

LIST OF ILLUSTRATIONS.

VOL. I.

The Look-Out

H.R.H. The Duke of Edinburgh

The "Great Harry" of 1488

One of Drake's Men

Battle Ship about 1650

One of Blake's Men

H.M.S. "Calliope"

Sailors (18th Century)

H.M.S. "Mohawk"

Admiral (18th Century)

H.M.S. "Magicienne"

Post-Captain (18th Century)

Battle Ship about 1760

Heaving the Lead (18th Century)

H.M.S. "Nymphe"

A 42-Gun Frigate about 1780

H.R.H. THE DUKE OF EDINBURGH.

THE "GREAT HARRY" OF 1488.

ONE OF DRAKE'S MEN, 1588.

BATTLE SHIP, ABOUT 1650.

ONE OF BLAKE'S MEN, 1650.

H.M.S. "CALLIOPE." 3rd CLASS CRUISER.

SAILORS

(18TH CENTURY).

HMS "MOHAWK" 3rd CLASS CRUISER.

ADMIRAL

(18TH CENTURY)

H.M.S. "MAGICIENNE." 2nd CLASS CRUISER.

POST CAPTAIN

(18TH CENTURY).

BATTLE SHIP, ABOUT 1760.

HEAVING THE LEAD.

(18TH CENTURY).

H.M.S. "NYMPHE" (SLOOP).

A 42-GUN FRIGATE, ABOUT 1780.

Her Majesty's Navy.

COASTGUARDSMAN

VOL. II.

HER MAJESTY'S NAVY

With Coloured Illustrations

By W. CHRISTIAN SYMONS and W. FRED. MITCHELL

VOLUME 2

LIST OF ILLUSTRATIONS.

VOL. II.

Coastguardsman

H.R.H. Prince George of Wales

A 38-Gun Frigate about 1770

H.M.S. "Bramble"

A 28-Gun Frigate about 1794

H.M.S. "Undaunted"

H.M.S. "Latona"

A 74-Gun Ship of the Line about 1794

H.M.S. "Colossus"

H.M.S. "Hero"

H.M.S. "Rodney"

Boatswain about 1829

H.M.S. "Victoria" (The Last of the Three-Deckers)

H.M.S. "Victoria"

H R H PRINCE GEORGE OF WALES.

A 38-GUN FRIGATE, ABOUT 1770

H. M. S. BRAMBLE.
1st class gunboat.

A 28-GUN FRIGATE, ABOUT 1794

H. M. S UNDAUNTED.
1ST CLASS CRUISER—BELTED.

H.M.S. LATONA.
2ND CLASS CRUISER.

A 74-GUN SHIP-OF-THE-LINE, ABOUT 1794.

H. M. S. COLOSSUS.
1ST CLASS BATTLE-SHIP.

H. M. S HERO.
2ND CLASS BATTLE-SHIP.

H.M.S. RODNEY.

1st CLASS BATTLE-SHIP.

BOATSWAIN

(About 1829).

H.M.S. VICTORIA, 121 guns.

(THE LAST THREE-DECKER—LAUNCHED IN 1859.)

H.M.S. VICTORIA.

1st CLASS BATTLE-SHIP.

Her Majesty's Navy.

LOWERING THE ENSIGN AT SUNSET.

VOL. III.

HER MAJESTY'S NAVY

With Coloured Illustrations

By W. Christian Symons and W. Fred. Mitchell

VOLUME 3

LIST OF ILLUSTRATIONS.

VOL. III.

Lowering the Ensign at Sunset

Lord Nelson

The "Victory"

"Captain"

A Boarding Party

H.M.S. "Thrush"

2nd Class Petty Officer

At the Breech-loading Gun

H.M.S. "Speedwell"

Signalling

Lieutenant and Signal Boy

Landing Order

H.M.S. "Blenheim"

Ship's Cook

H.M.S. "Royal Sovereign"

Royal Naval Artillery Volunteers

LORD NELSON.

THE VICTORY
(LAUNCHED 1765.)

CAPTAIN

A BOARDING PARTY.

H.M.S. THRUSH.
1st CLASS GUNBOAT.

2nd CLASS PETTY OFFICER.

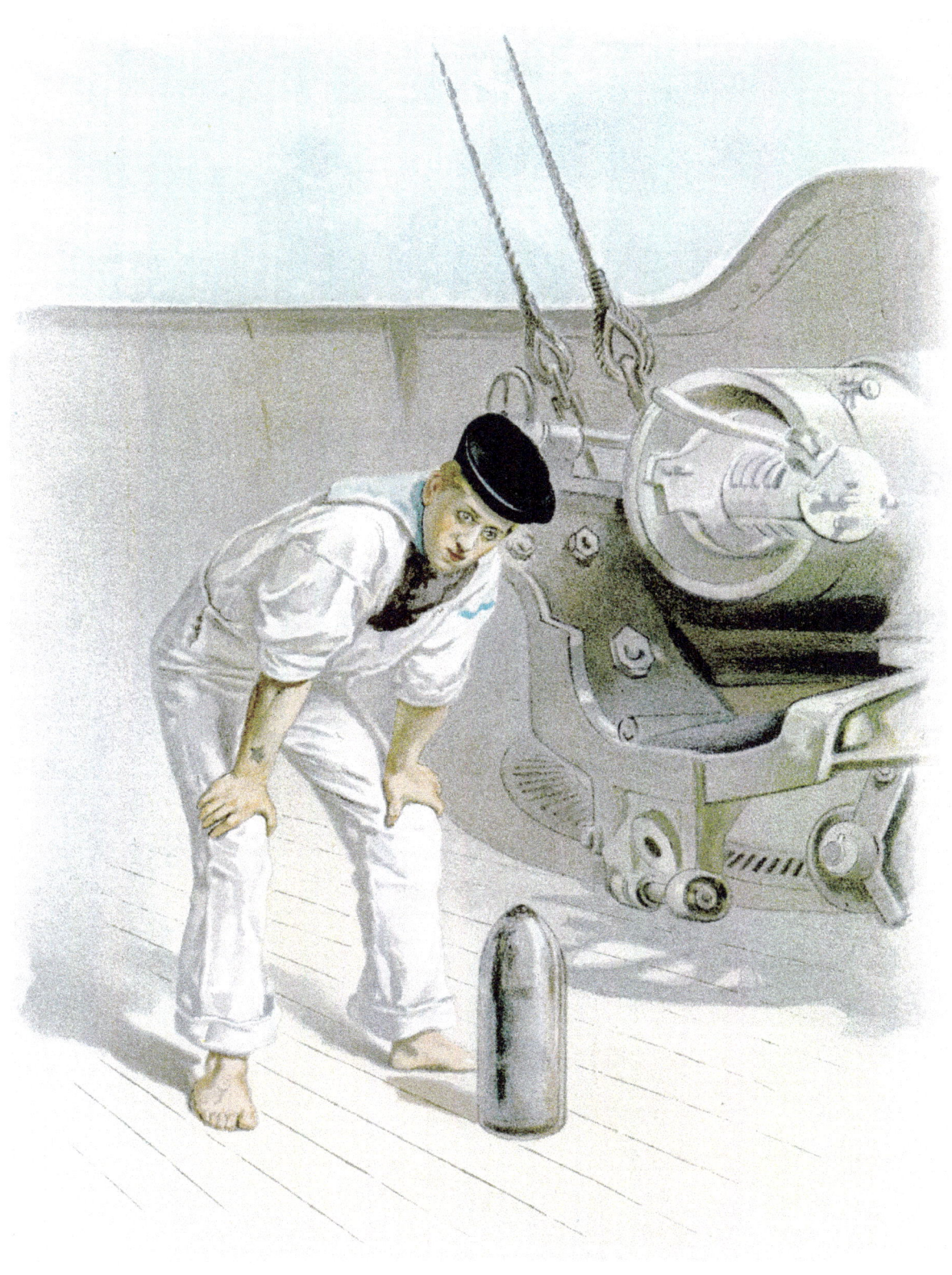

AT THE BREECHLOADING GUN.

H.M.S. SPEEDWELL.
TORPEDO GUNBOAT.

SIGNALLING.

LIEUTENANT AND SIGNAL BOY.

LANDING ORDER.

H.M.S. BLENHEIM.
1st CLASS CRUISER.

SHIP'S COOK.

H.M.S. ROYAL SOVEREIGN.

1ST CLASS. BATTLESHIP

ROYAL NAVAL ARTILLERY VOLUNTEER.

www.ingramcontent.com/pod-product-compliance
Lightning Source LLC
Chambersburg PA
CBHW060926170426
43192CB00025B/2904